This journal belongs to

To my dear friend Joyce, Thank you for being my inspiration. Love you Bernadette

Date: *Dec. 6 2023*

If you abide in me, and my words abide in you,
ask whatever you will, and it shall be done for you.

—John 15:7

"One day Jesus will ask each of us, 'Did you know me?' How we respond to that question will be determined by the depth of our prayer lives. *The Ave Prayer Intentions Journal* provides a great tool for deepening and accelerating your spiritual growth so that you can experience the adventure the saints raved about: intimacy with your Maker and the foretaste of eternal life."

Fr. David Michael Moses
Social media evangelist and founder of Pilgrim Rosary

"A person's prayer life is essentially his or her relationship with Jesus. Few people know where to turn to begin a prayer life of their own and fewer still know where to turn to deepen one. This prayer journal provides a strong skeleton of a prayer life for the reader to pack some muscle onto, for Jesus to then breathe his life into. For those wishing to bring their relationship with Jesus to life, I highly recommend using this!"

Tanner Kalina
Catholic speaker and TikTok evangelist

"This prayer intentions journal is a beautiful tool to deepen the most essential relationship in our lives, to actually *listen* to God speaking his love and goodness into our very hearts. Opening up to see what's on our hearts takes effort, thoughtfulness, and courage, but when we bring that vulnerability to God, he meets us there with abundance and allows us to encounter him as the fulfillment of all our greatest needs and desires."

Mariana Pimiento
Founder of Big Apple Catholic

"*The Ave Prayer Intentions Journal* is a true gift for a Catholic on the go. Packed with timeless wisdom from sacred scripture to the *Catechism* to the prayers of the saints, this little book will help countless souls pause and dive deeper into their prayer lives on a daily basis. It reminds us that prayer does not merely *help* our relationship with God but, rather, prayer *is* our relationship with God. I'm excited to put this to use in my own prayer life in the days and weeks to come."

Mark Hart
Chief Innovation Officer at Life Teen International

"Sometimes it feels like our prayer is locked inside us, or like our thoughts are so chaotically scattered that we'd be surprised if even God could figure them out! This journal can serve as a powerful first step in freeing us of confusions, inhibitions, and distractions to engage in real and life-changing conversations with the Lord."

Sr. Orianne Pietra René, FSP
Social media evangelist

The Ave
PRAYER INTENTIONS
Journal

A Record of My Conversations with God

Compiled by Heidi Hess Saxton

Ave Maria Press AVE Notre Dame, Indiana

Scripture quotations are from the *Revised Standard Version of the Bible—Second Catholic Edition (Ignatius Edition)*, copyright © 2006 National Council of the Churches of Christ in the United States of America. Used by permission. All rights reserved.

Prayer of St. Francis excerpted from "July 27" in *Through the Year with Francis of Assisi: Daily Meditations from His Words and Life*. Selected and translated by Murray Bodo, OFM, copyright © 1987 by Murray Bodo, OFM. Used by permission of Doubleday, an imprint of the Knopf Doubleday Publishing Group, a division of Penguin Random House LLC. All rights reserved.

© 2023 by Ave Maria Press, Inc.

All rights reserved. No part of this book may be used or reproduced in any manner whatsoever, except in the case of reprints in the context of reviews, without written permission from Ave Maria Press®, Inc., P.O. Box 428, Notre Dame, IN 46556, 1-800-282-1865.

Founded in 1865, Ave Maria Press is a ministry of the United States Province of Holy Cross.

www.avemariapress.com

Paperback: ISBN-13: 978-1-64680-259-3

E-book: ISBN-13: 978-1-64680-260-9

Cover image © martinussumbaji / iStock / Getty Images Plus.

Cover and text design by Samantha Watson.

Printed and bound in the United States of America.

CONTENTS

Introduction vii
Part One: My Prayers of Adoration and Blessing 1
Part Two: My Prayers of Contrition 23
Part Three: My Prayers of Thanksgiving and Praise 45
Part Four: My Prayers of Supplication 67
Part Five: My Prayers for the Faithful Departed 89
Part Six: My Daily Prayers 95
Part Seven: My Prayer Intentions 103

INTRODUCTION

> The Spirit helps us in our weakness; for we do not know how to pray as we ought, but the Spirit himself intercedes for us with sighs too deep for words. And he who searches the hearts of men knows what is the mind of the Spirit, because the Spirit intercedes for the saints according to the will of God.
> —Romans 8:26–27

Cultivating a life of prayer is the aspiration for every believer and the secret behind every saint because it keeps us rooted in the dynamic, life-giving love of God. Whether you have chosen to use this journal as a means to keep track of the people and situations for which you've promised to pray, or as a way to record your own thoughts and prayers as you are inspired, it will create a permanent record of your own spiritual journey, of your ongoing dialogue with God.

We may not know how to pray as we ought, as St. Paul writes, but if we set out with intentionality in our prayer, the Spirit will fill in the rest. According to St. Thérèse of Lisieux, prayer is simply "the raising of one's mind and heart to God or the requesting of good things from God." As people of faith, interceding for others is an important way to love them and share their concerns. This journal can help you organize the way you recall their needs—as well as your own—and invite God into your lives. By lifting our thoughts and concerns to God, we participate in an important way in God's plan of redemption for the whole world.

The first half of this journal contains prompts to jumpstart your prayer; the second half contains open pages for you to journal. Throughout, you will notice space to record how you have seen God respond to your prayers. Whether you return to these journal entries a day later or a year later, your faith will be strengthened as you recall God's creativity and faithfulness.

Four Types of Prayer

The *Catechism of the Catholic Church* identifies several fundamental forms of prayer that are important for our spiritual development (see *CCC* 2626–43):

- *Adoration*: Prayers of blessing and adoration place us in the presence of the Triune God—Father, Son, and Spirit—to acknowledge the greatness of the One who made us, the power of the One who sets us free from evil, and the blessing of the One who makes us holy.
- *Contrition*: In prayers of contrition we acknowledge our own weaknesses and limitations, and this enables us to approach God without shame or worry. These prayers deepen our trust in God's mercy, which acts like a spiritual shield to protect us against the "flaming darts of the Evil One" (Ephesians 6:16). While we embrace the graces of sacramental Confession for serious sin, prayers of contrition help us to be aware even of lesser faults that might distract or deter us from speaking with God heart-to-heart.
- *Thanksgiving*: Prayers of praise and thanksgiving express an awareness of God's many blessings, both those already received and those anticipated. Many of the saints, including Bl. Solanus Casey and St. Pio of Pietrelcina, urged those who came to them for prayer to thank God ahead of time for answered prayers. These prayers of thanksgiving, then, are a kind of catalyst of faith and trust that welcome the Holy Spirit into specific situations.
- *Supplication*: Prayers of supplication (also known as petition or intercession) are ways to invite God into our lives by asking for what we need. We might bring our own concerns forward, or concerns of people we love as well as those unknown to us, from the most immediate to the farthest reaching. These prayers might be for physical needs, such as financial or medical concerns, or they might be spiritual or relational in nature. The most powerful prayer of this type directly invites the Holy Spirit to come and accomplish God's will in that particular situation.

Adoration, contrition, thanksgiving, supplication—these fundamental types of Catholic prayer are easy to remember with the simple acronym "ACTS of faith." As we pray, we enter into a holy dialogue with God to better understand both the mystery of who he is and the reality of who we are in relation to him.

How Should I Pray?

Are you finding it difficult to find the right words to say or to write down? The prayers that have been handed down to us in our tradition can be a useful resource because we know generations of faithful people also found them helpful. You can find collections of prayers from our tradition in many sources—you can find some favorites in *The Ave Treasury of Catholic Prayers*. This inspirational resource can be used side-by-side with this journal, which gives you space to record your personal response to these timeless invocations.

However you choose to approach God—on your own or with the help of the saints—God hears us and has promised to answer. As we read in the Bible: "And this is the confidence which we have in him, that if we ask anything according to his will he hears us. And if we know that he hears us in whatever we ask, we know that we have obtained the requests made of him" (1 John 5:14–15).

How can we know if our petitions are "according to his will"? Here are some practical questions to ask yourself to help with this discernment.

- *Is any area of my life not fully surrendered to God?* Does your conscience point out areas of your life that are not aligned with God's plan as revealed in the scriptures? Ask God for the strength and humility to make things right.
- *Am I striving to get my own way in a particular situation?* Is there any situation in your life right now that you find difficult to entrust to God? God gave us the gift of free will, and he won't override our own stubbornness in order to accomplish his purposes. But when we ask him to take control of a situation and work all things for the ultimate good (see Romans 8:28), God can be trusted to answer those prayers—and transform us in the process.
- *Do I struggle with anxiety, fear, worry, or anger?* When these emotions take over our lives, it can be a sign that a kind of spiritual infection has taken root in the soul. But when we acknowledge them and offer them to God—and keep offering them each time they resurface—God will lighten our emotional load and give us "the peace of God, which passes all understanding" (Philippians 4:7).

Does God Really Listen to My Prayers?

When you think about God, what words come to mind most readily? As you consider suffering in the world—natural disasters, personal tragedies, and systemic injustices—are you sometimes tempted to think of God as impersonal, powerless, or capricious? Do you wonder what good your prayers might do? How can asking God for help accomplish anything at all?

The most persuasive answers to these questions are found in the person of Jesus, who teaches his followers throughout the gospels to regard God as Father. While this word can trouble those wounded by shortcomings in their own fathers, Jesus reveals God as the true Father who tenderly cares for his children. He offers this challenge in the Gospel of Matthew:

> Ask, and it will be given you; seek, and you will find; knock, and it will be opened to you. For every one who asks receives, and he who seeks finds, and to him who knocks it will be opened. Or what man of you, if his son asks him for bread, will give him a stone? Or if he asks for a fish, will give him a serpent? If you then, who are evil, know how to give good gifts to your children, how much more will your Father who is in heaven give good things to those who ask him?" (Matthew 7:7–11)

This journal is an open invitation for you to rediscover the fatherly nature of God—One who can be trusted and who listens, heals, forgives, restores, and provides. Over time, as you make note of all the blessings and graces God gives to you—including things you may not have thought to ask him for—these answered prayers will produce a harvest of rich spiritual fruit. As you return to him again and again with your ACTS of faith, you will be strengthened and assured of God's desire to hear and answer your prayers and to provide like any good Father for the things you need (see also Luke 11:13).

How to Use This Journal

This journal is arranged in seven parts. The first four parts are dedicated to the fundamental movements of prayer—the ACTS of faith. Each of these parts hold ten reflections with quotes and journal prompts to guide your prayer time.

Are you overwhelmed? Remind yourself of the greatness and mercy of God by turning to "Part One: My Prayers of Adoration and Blessing"—the Bible passages referenced there will call to mind the ways God accompanies each of us on our life's journey. Want to unburden something from your heart? Turn to "Part Two: My Prayers of Contrition." Are you grateful to God for his many blessings to you? Head over to "Part Three: My Prayers of Thanksgiving and Praise." Ready to storm heaven on behalf of a friend or loved one? Go to "Part Four: My Prayers of Supplication."

Part five of this journal will help you remember the faithful departed and pray for God to bring them to fullness of life in heaven. Part six offers room for you to record and write everyday prayers. Part seven gives you more room to write, journal, and record your dialogue with God alongside inspiring quotes from saints who have walked this way of faithfulness ahead of us.

Each time you take up this journal, take a moment to settle yourself in a quiet space and ask the Lord to speak to your heart. If distractions arise, simply release them and return to focusing on what God is saying in this moment. If a name or situation persists in your mind, make a brief note so you can come back to it later.

Next, decide what type of prayer you would like to focus on in that moment. Turn to a page in that section, and then reflect upon the journal prompts you find there in order to write your own prayerful exchange with the Lord. If you are finding it difficult to find the words you want to pray and would like a little inspiration, flip through the inspiring quotes and prayers in Part Seven, the traditional prayers of *The Ave Treasury of Catholic Prayers*, or turn in your Bible to the book of Psalms or the daily readings and meditate on the words you find there that spark something inside you, paying close attention to any specific phrases that resonate. Feel free to record meaningful passages such as these in this journal—both to help you commit the words to memory and so you can find them easily when you want to read them again.

When you are ready to begin writing your own prayer, don't worry about the quality of your writing or details like spelling and punctuation. (If it helps, you could consider jotting down some initial thoughts on a piece of scrap paper, then transferring the finished version into the journal as a place of permanent record.)

This is a safe place for you to reveal your innermost thoughts to God. As the Holy Spirit stirs up your thoughts in the coming days and weeks, feel free to return to what you've written to record any further insights or developments that may occur. This is just between you and God, so don't worry about finding the "right words" and know that you can express doubts or fears about what is happening. God knows it all—and loves you. Just tell him honestly about where you are right now. He's waiting to meet you, right where you are.

Above all, make this journal yours. There is no right or wrong way to use it—and if you fill it up, just write the beginning and ending dates in the front of your journal and start over with another one! Each volume represents a chapter in the book of your life, a precious record of your journey with Christ. Keep this journal handy as you read the Bible (or hear it proclaimed at Mass). Use the spaces provided to write down your own favorite quotes or insights and to reflect upon what God is saying to you through these words.

May the Lord bless you as you set out to cultivate a deeper life of prayer by joining the Spirit's work to "intercede for the saints according to the will of God" (Romans 8:27).

PART ONE
MY PRAYERS OF ADORATION AND BLESSING

I will extol you, my God and King,
and bless your name for ever and ever.
Every day I will bless you,
and praise your name for ever and ever.
Great is the Lord, and greatly to be praised,
and his greatness is unsearchable.
One generation shall laud your works to another,
and shall declare your mighty acts.
On the glorious splendor of your majesty,
and on your wondrous works, I will meditate.

—Psalm 145:1–5

Adoration and Blessing: Reflection One   Date:

> We adore you, O Christ, and we praise you,
> Because by your holy Cross you have redeemed the world.

This short verse, which is traditionally associated with the Stations of the Cross, evokes a great mystery of our faith: God saves us through his Son, Jesus Christ, who joined our humanity, even to the point of sharing our suffering and death. Through the Cross, he conquered death and raises us to new life. Such love is difficult to understand—yet Jesus waits for us to open our hearts to him. What do you want to say to him?

Lord Jesus, I adore you for . . .

For Pondering

How have I experienced God's redeeming love? How can I express my love for God today?

Lord, today I bless your name . . . O God who saves.

For God so loved the world that he gave his only-begotten Son, that whoever believes in him should not perish but have eternal life. For God sent the Son into the world, not to condemn the world, but that the world might be saved through him.

—John 3:16–17

Adoration and Blessing: Reflection Two   Date:

> Be still, and know that I am God.
> I am exalted among the nations.
> I am exalted in the earth!
> —Psalm 46:10

This verse from the Psalms speaks of God as the One who defends his people from evil and who causes wars to cease. In times of strife and conflict, we can place ourselves in God's presence and gain perspective. He sees and knows all that may be known, and he is actively working for our good. What do you want to say to him?

God, show me your greatness . . .

For Pondering

Where do I see God's greatness in the world today?

Lord, today I bless your name ... Almighty God.

You shall be a crown of beauty in the hand of the LORD,
    and a royal diadem in the hand of your God.
You shall no more be termed Forsaken,
    and your land shall no more be termed Desolate;
but you shall be called My delight is in her,
    and your land Married;
for the LORD delights in you.

—Isaiah 62:3–4

Adoration and Blessing: Reflection Three   Date:

> O come, let us worship and bow down,
> let us kneel before the Lord, our Maker!
> For he is God,
> and we are the people of his pasture,
> and the sheep of his hand.
> —Psalm 95:6–7

The image of Jesus as the Good Shepherd (see John 10:11–18) who cares for his sheep—seeking out those who have scattered and protecting those within the fold—evokes a powerful sense of the never-ending protection and care God has for us. How have you experienced this divine provision?

God, keep me close to you . . .

For Pondering

Where do I see God shepherding his people?

Lord, today I bless your name . . . O Lord, my shepherd.

The LORD is my shepherd, I shall not want;
    he makes me lie down in green pastures.
He leads me beside still waters;
    he restores my soul. . . .
Even though I walk through the valley
    of the shadow of death,
    I fear no evil;
for you are with me.

—Psalm 23:1–4

Part One: My Prayers of Adoration and Blessing

Adoration and Blessing: Reflection Four   Date:

> Yours, O Lord, is the greatness, and the power, and the glory, and the victory, and the majesty; for all that is in the heavens and in the earth is yours; yours is the kingdom, O Lord, and you are exalted as head above all.
> —1 Chronicles 29:11

This prayer of blessing from the lips of King David is uttered not at the height of his reign but shortly after God reveals that the task of building the Temple would not be entrusted to David but instead to his son, Solomon. These words of surrender and humility reveal the heart of one who is beloved by God and who loves and trusts God in return. David's example is a powerful reminder that each of us must surrender our most precious ambitions to God so that he might accomplish his purposes in us.

God, I adore you because . . .

For Pondering

What dreams and ambitions is God asking me to surrender to him today?

Lord, today I bless your name . . . God our provider.

I tell you, do not be anxious about your life, what you shall eat or what you shall drink, nor about your body, what you shall put on. Is not life more than food, and the body more than clothing? Look at the birds of the air: they neither sow nor reap nor gather into barns, and yet your heavenly Father feeds them. Are you not of more value than they?

—Matthew 16:25–26

Adoration and Blessing: Reflection Five   Date:

> You shall love the Lord your God with all your heart, and with all your soul, and with all your mind. This is the first and greatest commandment.
> —Matthew 22:37–38

Matthew's gospel records this as the response Jesus gave to the Pharisee who tested Jesus by asking him to name the greatest commandment. Love of God and love of neighbor, Jesus answered, are the two commandments that must inform all our actions and beliefs. Love alone breaks down pride, elevates our little sacrifices, and strengthens us to suffer what we must. In the eternal pilgrimage of life, love fuels us to reach our final destination.

God, I adore you for . . .

For Pondering

What do I need to do today out of love for God alone?

Lord, today I bless your name . . . O God of mercy.

Know therefore that the LORD your God is God, the faithful God who keeps covenant and merciful love with those who love him and keep his commandments, to a thousand generations.

—Deuteronomy 7:9

Adoration and Blessing: Reflection Six   Date:

> All-powerful, most holy, most high, supreme God,
> All good, highest good, holy good, who alone are good,
> Let us give you all praise, all glory, all thanks,
> All honor, all blessing, and all that is good.
> So be it. Amen.
> —Prayer of St. Francis

"Taste and see that the Lord is good," reads Psalm 34. David offered this prayer when he was facing adversity and fleeing an angry king—not an easy moment to feel like God is good. But God's goodness cannot be measured in terms of our personal comfort, for he works on our behalf for the good "in everything" (Romans 8:28). Even when we cannot perceive it, God's goodness can be trusted.

God, I bless you for . . .

For Pondering

Where do I see God's goodness in the world today?

Lord, today I bless your name . . . O God who delivers.

The LORD, your God, is in your midst,
    a warrior who gives victory;
he will rejoice over you with gladness,
    he will renew you in his love;
he will exult over you with loud singing.

—Zephaniah 3:17

Adoration and Blessing: Reflection Seven   Date:

> Blessed be the name of God for ever and ever,
> to whom belong wisdom and might. . . .
> He reveals deep and mysterious things;
> he knows what is in the darkness,
> and the light dwells with him.
> —Daniel 2:20, 22

Though he is living in captivity and in the service of a pagan king, Daniel turns to the "God of my fathers" (Daniel 2:23) for the wisdom and strength he needs to accomplish his appointed task. When we face what seems impossible, like Daniel, we can turn to the God who knows all, sees all, and gives wisdom to those who ask.

God, I bless your name . . .

For Pondering

Where do I need God's wisdom today?

Lord, today I bless your name . . . everlasting God.

Have you not known? Have you not heard?
The Lord is the everlasting God,
    the Creator of the ends of the earth.
He does not faint or grow weary,
    his understanding is unsearchable.
He gives power to the faint,
    and to him who has no might he increases strength. . . .
They who wait for the Lord shall renew their strength,
    they shall mount up with wings like eagles,
they shall run and not be weary,
    they shall walk and not faint.

—Isaiah 40:28–29, 31

Adoration and Blessing: Reflection Eight   Date:

> Therefore God has highly exalted him and bestowed on him the name which is above every name, that at the name of Jesus every knee should bow, in heaven and on earth and under the earth, and every tongue confess that Jesus Christ is Lord, to the glory of God the Father.
> —Philippians 2:9–11

"If you bear your cross willingly, it will carry you and lead you to your desired goal where suffering will end, but that cannot happen here," wrote Thomas à Kempis in his classic work, *The Imitation of Christ*. The humility of Christ, surrendering to the will of the Father even when this meant a humiliating and agonizing death on the Cross, led to the glory of the Resurrection. As we contemplate our share in his eternal life, we know we must follow in the humble steps of Jesus, whose love for the Father compelled him to surrender all.

God, grant me the humility to take up my own cross and follow you . . .

For Pondering

What form does my cross take today?

Lord, today I bless your name . . . O God of life.

Behold, I will open your graves, and raise you from your graves, O my people; and I will bring you home into the land of Israel. . . . And I will put my Spirit within you, and you shall live.

—Ezekiel 37:12, 14

Adoration and Blessing: Reflection Nine

Date:

> In many and various ways God spoke of old to our fathers by the prophets; but in these last days he has spoken to us by a Son. . . . He reflects the glory of God and bears the very stamp of his nature, upholding the universe by the word of his power.
> —Hebrews 1:1–3

Both the love and glory of the Father are found in the person of Jesus Christ, who comes to us, as often as we seek it, in the gift of the Eucharist. The more we spend time in his eucharistic presence, the more we reflect his glory in a world that is dying for light. As St. John Bosco wrote, "Whatever you do, think of the glory of God as your main goal. Have great confidence: God is always our Father, even when he sends us trials."

God, let me shine with your reflected glory . . .

For Pondering

How can I glorify Christ in my world today?

Lord, today I bless your name . . . O Light of the World.

I am the light of the world; he who follows me will not walk in darkness, but will have the light of life.

—John 8:12

Blessing and Adoration: Reflection Ten   Date:

> And I heard every creature in heaven and on earth and under the earth and in the sea, and all therein, saying, "To him who sits upon the throne and to the Lamb be blessing and honor and glory and might for ever and ever!"
> —Revelation 5:13

All creation fulfills its most elemental purpose in worshipping the Creator. Not because God needs our praise, but because we desperately need to be reminded of our place in the world. We are both stewards of the earth and children of heaven. We cannot accomplish one without acknowledging the other.

God, all creation declares your goodness . . .

For Pondering

How can I be a better steward of the earth?

Lord, today I bless your name ... Lord of all the earth, keeper of my soul.

I lift up my eyes to the hills.
　　From where does my help come?
My help comes from the Lord,
　　who made heaven and earth.
He will not let your foot be moved,
　　he who keeps you will not slumber.
The Lord is your keeper ...
The Lord will keep you from all evil;
　　he will keep your life.

—Psalm 121:1–5, 8

PART TWO
MY PRAYERS OF CONTRITION

Have mercy on me, O God,
according to your merciful love;
according to your abundant mercy blot out
my transgressions.
Wash me thoroughly from my iniquity,
and cleanse me from my sin!
For I know my transgressions,
and my sin is ever before me.
Against you, you only, have I sinned,
and done that which is evil in your sight. . . .
Behold, you desire truth in my inward being;
therefore teach me wisdom in my secret heart.
Purge me with hyssop, and I shall be clean;
wash me, and I shall be whiter than snow. . . .
Create in me a clean heart, O God,
and put a new and right spirit within me.

—Psalm 51:1–4, 6–7, 10

Contrition: Reflection One   Date:

> But he was wounded for our transgressions,
> he was bruised for our iniquities;
> upon him was the chastisement that made us whole,
> and with his stripes we are healed.
> —Isaiah 53:5

In these prayers of contrition, we speak with the Lord honestly about our faults and weaknesses, our own needs, in order to be "made whole" and so that we might be strong enough to carry others' burdens. When we feel broken—whether because of sin or because of circumstances in our lives—we can turn with confidence to the one true source of our healing, Jesus.

Lord Jesus, Great Physician, heal me . . .

For Pondering

In addition to any self-inflicted wounds of sin, am I harboring anger or resentment toward anyone else whose words or actions have been a cause of sorrow? I give those to Jesus, too.

Lord, so often I fall short of what I know I should be. Please help me do better. Today I am especially mindful of . . .

Contrition: Reflection Two   Date:

> Confess your sins to one another, and pray for one another, that you may be healed. The prayer of a righteous man has great power in its effects.
> —James 5:16–17

"Never confuse a single failure with a final defeat," wrote the great American author F. Scott Fitzgerald. Two steps forward and one step back—this is the human condition in a nutshell. When we recognize our own areas of vulnerability (rather than trying to hide our faults), the bonds of pride are broken, making room for the Spirit to move, to restore, and to transform.

I'm sorry, Lord, because . . .

For Pondering

When I approach the sacrament of Confession and reflect on my life, what are the habits and patterns of my life that tend to lead me into the same sins?

Lord, you see the sins that tempt me most. Deliver me, O Lord, from . . .

Contrition: Reflection Three   Date:

> A new heart I will give you, and a new spirit I will put within you;
> and I will take out of your flesh the heart of stone and give you
> a heart of flesh. And I will put my spirit with in you.
> —Ezekiel 36:26–27a

In his *Introduction to the Devout Life*, St. Francis de Sales observes: "When little bees are caught in a storm, they take hold of small stones so they can keep their balance when they fly. Our firm resolution to stay with God is like stability to the soul amid the rolling waves of life." Clinging to God gives us strength to stay on course, even when our failings—or the failings of others—threaten to trip us up. Without God as an anchor, we harden our hearts against those whose failings mirror our own, and we succumb to judgment and lack of compassion.

Forgive me, Lord, for . . .

For Pondering

Is there someone in my life whom I struggle to love, or with whom I am frequently impatient? This is someone Christ loves—I will ask him to show me how to love this person, too.

Lord, take this stone from my heart, and give me a heart of compassion, for . . .

Contrition: Reflection Four   Date:

> My little children, your hearts are small, but prayer stretches them and makes them capable of loving God. Through prayer we receive a foretaste of heaven and something of paradise comes down to us.
> —St. John Vianney

Do you hunger to spend time with God? Do you respond eagerly when you sense God's presence, like a distant friend who unexpectedly makes an appearance at your doorstep? If not—if prayer feels like an arduous duty, rather than a delightful pastime—what is occupying that place in your heart?

Lord Jesus, make me hungry for your presence . . .

For Pondering

Throughout our lives, we may experience moments of spiritual awakening that make us especially aware of the things of God. Gradually, over time, this feeling may wane, and the love we once felt mellows into something deeper and more permanent. How would I characterize my relationship with God now? What would I like it to be?

Read the verse at the bottom of this page. Do these biblical images for Jesus ring true for you? How and when do you experience him in each way? What are other titles you could give to the ways he comes to you?

Lord, you are my Bread of Life.
You are my Living Water.
You are the Way, Truth, and Life.
You are . . .

Contrition: Reflection Five   Date:

> Come to me, all who labor and are heavy laden, and I will give you rest. Take my yoke upon you, and learn from me; for I am gentle and lowly in heart, and you will find rest for your souls. For my yoke is easy, and my burden is light.
> —Matthew 11:28–29

"If God gives you the burden, God will give you the strength," said St. Josemaria Escriva. When we are honest with God about the weight we are carrying, he never fails to fortify us with the strength we need, as we need it. Stay in the present, and in his Presence. You will receive what you need.

Lord Jesus, I confess I need you today for . . .

For Pondering

When we try to hide our burdens or failings from others or from God, their weight becomes heavier. And yet, is there anything I could say that God does not already know about me? What makes me fearful to name these things? I will practice giving God my fear, so I may find the courage to give him everything else.

Lord, please take away this burden from me, and bring me to the light . . .

Contrition: Reflection Six   Date:

> Have nothing to do with godless and silly myths. Train yourself in godliness; for while bodily training is of some value, godliness is of value in every way, as it holds promise for the present life and also for the life to come.
> —1 Timothy 4:7–8

Have you grown "spiritually flabby" by acquiring habits that align with cultural values, rather than God's revealed truth? Consider what you read and view, how you spend your time, and how you spend your money. What do these things say about your priorities?

Lord Jesus, reveal to me the truth about myself . . . Am I spiritually fit?

For Pondering

If I were to welcome Jesus into my home for a weekend, is there anything I would need to change or reschedule for his comfort as well as my own?

Lord, come and make your home in my heart and in my living space. Show me what I need to change to be more like you.

Contrition: Reflection Seven

Date:

> Too late have I loved you, O Beauty so ancient, O Beauty so new. Too late have I loved you! You were within me but I was outside myself, and there I sought you! In my weakness I ran after the beauty of the things you have made. You were with me, and I was not with you. The things you have made kept me from you—the things which would have no being unless they existed in you! You have called, you have cried, and you have pierced my deafness.
> —St. Augustine

To be awakened by beauty is to become keenly aware of one of the greatest of all spiritual mysteries: the boundless creative genius of God and his infinite capacity to love us. As we perceive such goodness, beauty, and truth, we are driven to our knees by the knowledge of how short of these ideals we fall. This honesty and humility is the first step on the road to holiness.

Lord Jesus, I am blinded by selfishness and sin. Reveal to me the beauty of your heart . . .

For Pondering

Where do I experience the beauty of the Lord most profoundly?

Lord, open my eyes, unstop my ears, awaken my heart . . .

Part Two: My Prayers of Contrition

Contrition: Reflection Eight   Date:

> God is light and in him is no darkness at all. If we say we have fellowship with him while we walk in darkness, we lie and do not live according to the truth; but if we walk in the light, as he is in the light, we have fellowship with one another, and the blood of Jesus his Son cleanses us from all sin.
> —1 John 1:5b–7

Padre Pio once wrote, "In darkness, times of tribulation, and spiritual anxiety, Jesus is with you. In that state, you see nothing but darkness in your spirit, but I assure you, on behalf of God, that the light of the Lord invades and surrounds your entire spirit." That light may be insensible to us right in this moment—but hold on with faith that dawn is coming.

Lord Jesus, in your mercy shine your light in my darkness . . .

For Pondering

How have I closed my eyes or turned away from the light of truth in my life, deliberately putting myself in darkness?

Lord, as I reflect on this prayer from St. John Henry Newman (see below), help me better understand the gloom that darkens my way, the light you are bringing, and the next step forward . . .

Lead, kindly light, amid the circling gloom,
Lead thou me on;
The night is dark and I am far from home,
Lead thou me on!
Keep thou my feet;
I do not ask to see the distant scene.
One step enough for me.

Contrition: Reflection Nine   Date:

> Humble yourselves therefore under the mighty hand of God, that in due time he may exalt you. Cast all your anxieties on him, for he cares about you.
> —1 Peter 5:6–7

"Sometimes the only way the good Lord can get into some hearts is to break them," wrote Ven. Fulton Sheen. When the weight of shame is heavy, and pride tempts us to hide, shift blame, or rationalize our actions, let us come like children to our loving Father. He always stands ready to make things right.

Lord Jesus, let me tell you what is weighing me down right now . . .

For Pondering

Anger can often be symptomatic of deflected guilt or wounded pride. In the Our Father we pray, "Forgive us . . . as we forgive." Have I hurt anyone with anger? What is at the root of that emotion for me? How can I show mercy to myself and others?

Lord, thank you for working in these difficulties to teach me humility . . .

Contrition: Reflection Ten   Date:

> And I saw the holy city, new Jerusalem, coming down out of heaven from God . . . and I heard a great voice from the throne saying, "Behold, the dwelling of God is with men. He will dwell with them . . . he will wipe away every tear from their eyes, and death shall be no more, neither shall there be mourning nor crying nor pain any more, for the former things have passed away. . . . Behold, I make all things new."
> —Revelation 21:2–5a

To be a Christian is to be keenly aware of our own mortality—the fact that our time on earth is fleeting and we must do good while we can. We don't have forever to return to God—death will come for us at an unexpected hour, and one day the Lord will come again at the end of time. Despite our failings, we live with hope because we believe in God's power to make all things new. And so we pray with all Christians in every time and place: *Maranatha!* Come, Lord Jesus!

Lord Jesus, let me be ready to receive you and to live with heaven in mind . . .

For Pondering

If I knew Jesus were returning to earth tomorrow to bring forth the kingdom of God, what would I need to do today?

Lord, no one is guaranteed tomorrow. How can I live for you today? . . .

PART THREE
MY PRAYERS OF THANKSGIVING AND PRAISE

I give you thanks, O Lord, with my whole heart;
before the angels I sing your praise;
I bow down toward your holy temple
and give thanks to your name for your
mercy and your faithfulness;
for you have exalted above everything
your name and your word. . . .
Though I walk in the midst of trouble,
you preserve my life;
you stretch out your hand against
the wrath of my enemies,
and your right hand delivers me.
The Lord will fulfil his purpose for me;
your mercy, O Lord, endures for ever.
Do not forsake the work of your hands.

—Psalm 138:1–2, 7–8

Thanksgiving and Praise: Reflection One   Date:

> May God be gracious to us and bless us
> and make his face to shine upon us,
> that your way may be known upon earth,
> your saving power among all nations.
> Let the peoples praise you, O God;
> let all the peoples praise you!
> —Psalm 67:1–3

This hymn praises God's mercy and nearness as good news to be shared with all nations of the world—not just among those whom he has chosen for himself. As Christians, we recognize the fullness of this revelation of mercy in Jesus Christ, who sent his followers out into the world to preach the Gospel to every nation (see Matthew 28:18–20).

God, I thank you for all you have done for me, and I praise you for who you are . . .

For Pondering

We thank God to acknowledge the blessings he gives to enrich our lives. But why do we need to praise God? "Praise embraces the other forms of prayer and carries them toward him who is the source and goal, the 'one God, the Father, from whom are all things and for whom we exist'" (*CCC* 2638; 1 Corinthians 8:6). How can I praise God today?

Lord, thank you for . . .

And I praise you for . . .

If you wish, write a brief hymn or prayer of praise to the Lord for his goodness to you and those you love.

Thanksgiving and Praise: Reflection Two

Date:

> For he will deliver you from the snare of the fowler
> and from the deadly pestilence;
> he will cover you with his pinions,
> and under his wings you will find refuge;
> his faithfulness is a shield and buckler.
> —Psalm 91:3–4

"Protected, covered, and defended by the uniform of this dear Lord, let us stand before him and pray with the humility of the creature and the confidence and freedom of a child," wrote Padre Pio. "And given that God loves to delight in us, let nothing in the world distract us from delighting in him and contemplating his grandeur." How have you experienced this protection?

God, you are my deliverer. I praise you for your everlasting protection . . .

For Pondering

The Bible conveys God's attributes with images from nature (a refuge, a rock, references to wings, etc.). What images would I use to describe God's protection?

Lord, thank you for . . .

And I praise you for . . .

If you wish, write a brief hymn or prayer of praise to the Lord for his protection and faithfulness to you and those you love.

Part Three: My Prayers of Thanksgiving and Praise

Thanksgiving and Praise: Reflection Three   Date:

> The LORD is the strength of his people,
> he is the saving refuge of his anointed.
> O save your people, and bless your heritage;
> be their shepherd, and carry them for ever.
> —Psalm 28:8–9

Pope Benedict XVI observed, "God 'comes': he comes to be with us in every situation of ours, he comes to dwell among us, to live with us and within us; he comes to fill the gaps that divide and separate us; he comes to reconcile us with him and with one another." By his Spirit, God moves from person to person, home to home, and community to community, seeking hearts that are joined in praise.

God, I lift my heart to rejoice in your goodness . . .

For Pondering

How can I work and pray for unity in my own family and community?

50   *The Ave Prayer Intentions Journal*

Lord, thank you for . . .

And I praise you for . . .

If you wish, write a brief hymn or prayer of praise to the Lord for his goodness to your family or community.

Thanksgiving and Praise: Reflection Four   Date:

> But ask the beasts, and they will teach you;
> the birds of the air, and they will tell you;
> or the plants of the earth, and they will teach you;
> and the fish of the sea will declare to you.
> Who among all these does not know
> that the hand of the Lord has done this?
> In his hand is the life of every living thing
> and the breath of all mankind.
> —Job 12:7–10

Some days the buzz and gleam of the ever-present digital world begin to wear on us, and we need to return to the basic goodness of God's creation. Walk on the beach or through the woods. Get on the ground and play with kids or a puppy. Connecting with nature, and giving thanks to God for his creative genius, is a beautiful way to fortify prayer with simple delight.

God, I praise you for . . .

For Pondering

Where have I seen glimpses of God's goodness and creative artistry today?

Lord, thank you for . . .

And I praise you for . . .

If you wish, write a brief hymn or prayer of praise to the Lord for his greatness, as you've seen in nature.

Thanksgiving and Praise: Reflection Five   Date:

> We give thanks to God always for you all, constantly mentioning you in our prayers, remembering before our God and Father your work of faith and labor of love and steadfastness of hope in our Lord Jesus Christ.
> —1 Thessalonians 1:2–3

From the moment he created the first human being, God acknowledged that "it is not good that the man should be alone; I will make him a helper fit for him" (Genesis 2:18). Each of us needs the assistance and influence of others to become the person God wants us to be. Whom has God placed in your life to help you toward heaven? Why not give thanks and praise to God for them today?

God, I praise and thank you for the gift of love I have experienced through these people . . .

For Pondering

How am I positively influencing the lives of others to perpetuate this legacy of love?

Lord, thank you for . . .

And I praise you for . . .

If you wish, write a brief hymn or prayer of praise to the Lord for people who have helped you grow in faith, hope, and love.

Thanksgiving and Praise: Reflection Six   Date:

> For the LORD will build up Zion,
> he will appear in his glory;
> he will regard the prayer of the destitute,
> and will not despise their supplication.
> Let this be recorded for a generation to come,
> so that a people yet unborn may praise the Lord.
> —Psalm 102:16–18

In times of need we turn to God, who often answers our prayers in unexpected ways. Whether we encounter spiritual or physical poverty, we know God is close to us. Perhaps he is reaching out to us through the people in our lives. Today we praise the Lord who does not abandon us, but provides for us in our hour of need.

God, thank you for your generosity. I praise you for your care for me in my need . . .

For Pondering

Jesus promises that the kingdom of heaven belongs to the "poor in spirit" (Matthew 5:3). What advantage does powerlessness convey to those seeking God's reign? How am I in need of God?

Lord, thank you for . . .

And I praise you for . . .

If you wish, write a brief hymn or prayer of praise to the Lord for his mercy toward you when you were powerless.

Thanksgiving and Praise: Reflection Seven   Date:

> Let us then with confidence draw near to the throne of grace, that we may receive mercy and find grace to help in time of need.
> —Hebrews 4:16

"There are three things . . . by which faith stands firm, devotion remains constant, and virtue endures. They are prayer, fasting, and mercy," explained St. Peter Chrysologus. Each time we extend mercy to others, however imperfectly, we reflect what we have first received: the infinite mercy of God.

God, I praise you for your infinite mercy . . .

For Pondering

How am I experiencing the mercy of God right now? How is God calling me to extend that mercy to others?

Lord, thank you for . . .

And I praise you for . . .

If you wish, write a brief hymn or prayer of praise to the Lord for his patience when you or others have resisted his mercy.

Thanksgiving and Praise: Reflection Eight   Date:

> Have no anxiety about anything, but in everything by prayer and supplication with thanksgiving let your requests be made known to God. And the peace of God, which passes all understanding, will keep your hearts and your minds in Christ Jesus.
> —Philippians 4:6–7

Do you have a tendency to worry or be anxious? Praise is often an effective way to anchor an anxious heart. Tell God how you are feeling, and begin to recount the ways he has met your needs in the past. Speak the truth of who God is, and trust in his providence. Even the smallest step of faith will break the bonds of worry and lead you closer to the heart of the Father.

God, thank you for your faithfulness to me . . .

For Pondering

What is a concern that is preoccupying my thoughts right now—one I feel called to give over to God? How can I turn this worry into an opportunity for thankfulness and praise?

Lord, thank you for . . .

And I praise you for . . .

If you wish, write a brief hymn or prayer of praise to the Lord for his providing love.

Thanksgiving and Praise: Reflection Nine   Date:

> For I am sure that neither death, nor life, nor angels, nor principalities, nor things present, nor things to come, nor powers, nor height, nor depth, nor anything else in all creation, will be able to separate us from the love of God in Christ Jesus our Lord.
> —Romans 8:38

Do you sometimes feel that there is a great barrier between you and God, that your prayers are bouncing off the ceiling unheard? No matter what we are feeling, the truth is that there is nothing in all creation that can keep us from God. Even sin, which can break down the lines of communication, can be remedied quickly the moment we confess our sin and return to God, trusting in his mercy. The love of God is the most powerful force in the universe!

God, thank you for your amazing love, which never lets me go . . .

For Pondering

Am I sometimes tempted to move away from God? What is causing that sense of separation? What do I need to do to restore my connection to that infinite source of love?

Lord, thank you for . . .

And I praise you for . . .

If you wish, write a brief hymn or prayer of praise to the Lord for his love of all humanity.

Thanksgiving and Praise: Reflection Ten

Date:

> I heard a great voice from the throne saying, "Behold, the dwelling of God is with men. He will dwell with them, and they shall be his people, and God himself will be with them; he will wipe away every tear from their eyes, and death shall be no more . . . for the former things have passed away."
> —Revelation 21:3–4

Among the last words Jesus spoke to his disciples was the promise that "I go to prepare a place for you" (John 14:2b)—and he promises this for us as well. When those we love precede us in death, the pain is real and deep. Yet even this grief and loss can be offered to God with praise and thanksgiving because we know that we will see our loved ones again when we are united with God in heaven. In the meantime, prayer forms a lasting bond that keeps us united as one body, visible and invisible.

God, I thank you for the promise of heaven, and I praise you for the glories yet to come . . .

For Pondering

Whom do I most hope to encounter in heaven? Who needs my prayers to assist them heavenward?

Lord, thank you for . . .

And I praise you for . . .

If you wish, write a brief hymn or prayer of praise to the Lord in anticipation of all he is preparing for us in heaven.

PART FOUR
MY PRAYERS OF SUPPLICATION

O Lord, how manifold are your works!
In wisdom you have made them all;
the earth is full of your creatures.
Yonder is the sea, great and wide,
which teems with things innumerable,
living things both small and great. . . .
These all look to you,
to give them their food in due season.
When you give to them, they gather it up;
when you open your hand,
they are filled with good things.
When you hide your face, they are dismayed;
when you take away their spirit, they die
and return to their dust.
When you send forth your Spirit, they are created;
and you renew the face of the earth.

—Psalm 104:24–25, 27–30

Prayer of Supplication: Reflection One   Date:

> [Jesus said:] "If you abide in me, and my words abide in you, ask whatever you will, and it shall be done for you. By this my Father is glorified, that you bear much fruit, and so prove to be my disciples."
> —John 15:7–8

These two verses uniquely capture the job description of an effective intercessor. Our primary task is to abide in Christ—to listen intently to the Word of God so that every thought, word, and deed becomes oriented like a compass toward eternity. This clarifies our vision so we can see and pray for what is truly needed for ourselves and others. Abiding in Christ is the way of fruitful prayer and of lifelong discipleship.

Word of God, Jesus Christ, let me never lose sight of you . . .

For Pondering

Is God truly the guiding force of my life? How have I experienced this? What are the needs God is surfacing in my heart for me to pay attention to?

Lord, today I want to bring to you . . .

Lord, I want to thank you for your many blessings in my life and for answered prayers of the past . . .

Jesus, I trust in you. Here are some difficult situations I don't know how to pray for. Please send your Spirit to intercede, that God's will might be accomplished . . .

Prayer of Supplication: Reflection Two   Date:

> Let me hear what God the Lord will speak,
> for he will speak peace to his people,
> to his saints, to those who turn to him in their hearts.
> Surely his salvation is at hand for those who fear him,
> that glory may dwell in our land.
> —Psalm 85:8–9

"A faith that does not trouble us is a troubled faith," observed Pope Francis. "A faith that does not make us grow is a faith that needs to grow. A faith that does not raise questions is a faith that has to be questioned. A faith that does not shake us is a faith that needs to be shaken." As we look around us and see the divisions and conflict in the Church and the world, we continue to pray for the Spirit of peace to work in our hearts, healing and restoring God's people and bringing peace to our land.

God, turn my heart to you. By your power, protect, restore, and heal me so that I might be a source of light and hope to the world.

For Pondering

What are some of the root causes of division and conflict in my family, community, the Church, our nation, and in the world today? Where is the peace of God needed most? How might I help offer that peace?

Lord, today I want to bring to you . . .

Lord, I want to thank you for your many blessings in my life and for answered prayers of the past . . .

Jesus, I trust in you. Here are some difficult situations I don't know how to pray for. Please send your Spirit to intercede, that God's will might be accomplished . . .

Prayer of Supplication: Reflection Three   Date:

> Most of our life is unimportant, filled with trivial things from morning till night. But when it is transformed by love it is of interest even to the angels.
> —Dorothy Day

The ongoing, protective presence of our angels helps us as they guide even our humblest, simplest acts of prayer toward heaven throughout the day. As Psalm 81 reminds us, "For he will give his angels charge of you, to guard you in all your ways." What would you like to entrust to your guardian angel today?

God, let the words of my mouth and the work of my hands please you . . .

For Pondering

As I think about the past day, is there anything I wish I had not said or done? Or is there any act of prayer or love that, in retrospect, I can entrust to my guardian angel as a special offering to God?

Lord, today I want to bring to you . . .

Lord, I want to thank you for your many blessings in my life and for answered prayers of the past . . .

Jesus, I trust in you. Here are some difficult situations I don't know how to pray for. Please send your Spirit to intercede, that God's will might be accomplished . . .

Prayer of Supplication: Reflection Four   Date:

> Gladness of heart is the life of man,
> and the rejoicing of a man is length of days.
> Delight your soul and comfort your heart,
> and remove sorrow far from you,
> for sorrow has destroyed many,
> and there is no profit in it.
> —Sirach 30:22–23

The words we speak reveal the orientation of our hearts (see Matthew 12:34). And so our prayers reveal to a great degree whether we are focused primarily on self-interest or on humility and detachment—two virtues that St. Teresa of Avila identified as most essential to the life of faith because they depend upon trust in God. What do the words you have spoken today reveal about your disposition?

God, help me rejoice today—be my delight and my comfort . . .

For Pondering

How am I experiencing "gladness of heart"? How is my life marked by sorrow?

Lord, today I want to bring to you . . .

Lord, I want to thank you for your many blessings in my life and for answered prayers of the past . . .

Jesus, I trust in you. Here are some difficult situations I don't know how to pray for. Please send your Spirit to intercede, that God's will might be accomplished . . .

Prayer of Supplication: Reflection Five   Date:

> May the God of steadfastness and encouragement grant you to live in such harmony with one another, in accord with Christ Jesus, that together you may with one voice glorify the God and Father of our Lord Jesus Christ.
> —Romans 15:5

"Lord, open our eyes, that we may see you in our brothers and sisters," prayed St. Teresa of Calcutta. "Lord, open our ears, that we may hear the cries of the hungry, the cold, the frightened, the oppressed. Lord, open our hearts, that we may love each other as you love us. Renew us in your spirit, Lord, and make us one." How might you take this prayer for unity to heart?

God, make me an instrument of unity in the world today . . .

For Pondering

Sometimes it is those in closest proximity to us who are hardest to love. Whom am I being called to love more deeply?

Lord, today I want to bring to you . . .

Lord, I want to thank you for your many blessings in my life and for answered prayers of the past . . .

Jesus, I trust in you. Here are some difficult situations I don't know how to pray for. Please send your Spirit to intercede, that God's will might be accomplished . . .

Part Four: My Prayers of Supplication

Prayer of Supplication: Reflection Six

Date:

> First of all, then, I urge that supplications, prayers, intercessions, and thanksgivings be made for all men, for kings and all who are in high positions, that we may lead a quiet and peaceable life, godly and respectful in every way.
> —1 Timothy 2:1–2

At the 1968 World Council of Churches, Orthodox Patriarch Ignatius spoke of the actions of the Holy Spirit in the world: "Without the Holy Spirit, God is far away. Christ stays in the past, the gospel is simply an organization, authority is a matter of propaganda, the liturgy is no more than an evolution, Christian love a slave mentality," he said. "But *in the Holy Spirit*, the cosmos is resurrected and grows with the birth pangs of the kingdom. The Risen Christ is there, the gospel is the power of life, the Church shows forth the life of the Trinity, authority is a liberating science, mission is a Pentecost, the Liturgy is both renewal and anticipation, human action is deified." How do you see the Holy Spirit at work in your life?

Come, Holy Spirit! Renew me . . .

For Pondering

Have I prayed for the Holy Spirit to be unleashed in my corner of the world? Where is his presence most needed right now?

Lord, today I want to bring to you . . .

Lord, I want to thank you for your many blessings in my life and for answered prayers of the past . . .

Jesus, I trust in you. Here are some difficult situations I don't know how to pray for. Please send your Spirit to intercede, that God's will might be accomplished . . .

Prayer of Supplication: Reflection Seven   Date:

> Let us hold fast the confession of our hope without wavering, for he who promised is faithful; and let us consider how to stir up one another to love and good works, not neglecting to meet together, as is the habit of some, but encouraging one another, and all the more as you see the Day drawing near.
> —Hebrews 10:23–25

"Martyrdom is small, hidden, misunderstood," wrote Dorothy Day about the gift of perseverance. "It is the cry in the dark, the terror, the shame, the loneliness, nobody to hear, nobody to suffer with, let alone to save. Oh, the loneliness of all of us in these days, in all the great moments of our lives, this dying which we do, by little and by little, over a short space of time or over the years." When have you experienced desolation and loneliness in your need? Who needs your encouragement today?

God, you see my weakness. Strengthen me with the courage and diligence to persevere . . .

For Pondering

If I believe God is faithful, what can make my hope waver? In what ways are others I know experiencing a loss of hope—and what do *they* need to believe God is faithful?

Lord, today I want to bring to you . . .

Lord, I want to thank you for your many blessings in my life and for answered prayers of the past . . .

Jesus, I trust in you. Here are some difficult situations I don't know how to pray for. Please send your Spirit to intercede, that God's will might be accomplished . . .

Prayer of Supplication: Reflection Eight   Date:

> And [Jesus] told them a parable, to the effect that they ought always to pray and not lose heart.
> —Luke 18:1

Do you ever go back to God with the same prayer, over and over, and wonder if he isn't answering out of sheer annoyance? The parable of the unjust judge (see Luke 18:1–8) offers reassurance. Even when other people get tired of listening to us, God wants to listen. John Newton, the abolitionist who wrote the hymn "Amazing Grace," said, "Remember, the growth of a believer is not like a mushroom but like an oak, which increases slowly indeed, but surely. Many suns, showers, and frosts pass upon it before it comes to perfection. And in winter, when it seems to be dead, it is gathering strength at the root. Be humble, watchful, and diligent . . . fix your eyes upon Jesus and all will be well."

God, hear the cries of my heart. Shower me with your mercy . . .

For Pondering

Is my faith more like a mushroom, spreading through undergrowth, or an acorn reaching for the sky? Or something else?

Lord, today I want to bring to you . . .

Lord, I want to thank you for your many blessings in my life and for answered prayers of the past . . .

Jesus, I trust in you. Here are some difficult situations I don't know how to pray for. Please send your Spirit to intercede, that God's will might be accomplished . . .

Prayer of Supplication: Reflection Nine   Date:

> Hear my prayer, O Lord;
> give ear to my supplications!
> In your faithfulness answer me,
> in your righteousness! . . .
> I remember the days of old,
> I meditate on all that you have done;
> I muse on what your hands have wrought.
> I stretch out my hands to you;
> my soul thirsts for you like a parched land.
> —Psalm 143:1, 5–6

Looking back to see God's faithfulness gives us confidence in his loving care for us. Spend a few moments browsing the past pages of this journal and meditate on all that God has done with you. What do you notice about the concerns you recorded? How has God been faithful to you in those situations? Trusting in God's goodness, stretch out your hands to him and offer the needs and concerns you are carrying.

God, I meditate on the goodness your hands have wrought in my life . . .

For Pondering

God our Father loves each of us as his own child and is not too busy for the concerns we have. If I were to share everything that is weighing me down, without filtering what I think is worthy of his attention, what would I offer?

Lord, today I want to bring to you . . .

Lord, I want to thank you for your many blessings in my life and for answered prayers of the past . . .

Jesus, I trust in you. Here are some difficult situations I don't know how to pray for. Please send your Spirit to intercede, that God's will might be accomplished . . .

Prayer of Supplication: Reflection Ten   Date:

> My soul magnifies the Lord,
> and my spirit rejoices in God my Savior . . .
> for he who is mighty has done great things for me,
> and holy is his name.
> —Luke 1:46–47, 49

Mary was the first person Jesus saw when his eyes opened on the world, and she was likely the last he saw as he breathed out his final breath from the Cross, having entrusted her to his beloved disciple and to all of us. Mary enfolds within her mantle those who trust in her care. When we turn to her for help, she never fails to bring us to her Son.

Holy Mary, Mother of God, pray for us, now and at the hour of death . . .

For Pondering

When confronted with the unusual and mysterious way in which Jesus's birth came about, Mary reflectively kept this and the subsequent events of her life close, "pondering them in her heart" (Luke 2:19). As our mother in faith, she calls us to ponder what God is doing in our lives. How can I do so in my daily prayer?

Mary, Our Lady, help me bring the love of your Son, Jesus, into these situations that need it . . .

Mother Mary, here are some difficult situations I don't know how to pray for. Please pray for me, that God's will might be accomplished . . .

PART FIVE
MY PRAYERS FOR THE FAITHFUL DEPARTED

The souls of the righteous are in the hand of God,
and no torment will ever touch them.
In the eyes of the foolish they seemed to have died,
and their departure was thought to be an affliction,
and their going from us to be their destruction;
but they are at peace.
For though in the sight of men they were punished,
their hope is full of immortality.
Having been disciplined a little, they will receive great good,
because God tested them and found them worthy of himself;
like gold in the furnace he tried them. . . .
Those who trust in him will understand truth,
and the faithful will abide with him in love,
because grace and mercy are upon his elect,
and he watches over his holy ones.

—Wisdom 3:1–6a, 9

Prayers for the Dead

> Therefore, since we are surrounded by so great a cloud of witnesses, let us also lay aside every weight, and sin which clings so closely, and let us run with perseverance the race that is set before us.
> —Hebrews 12:1

While running or at rest, our gaze must remain on Jesus. The saints kept their eyes on the Lord until the end. Their prayers encourage us as we make our way toward our finish line. And by remembering in our own prayers those who are dying and the faithful departed who precede us, we urge them on in their final journey toward heaven. Our communion with those who have died—this "great cloud of witnesses"—keeps our eyes focused on our final destination: union with God.

These are the names of those who have died. In remembering them here, I entrust them to the merciful love of Jesus Christ, who suffered, died, and rose to bring us eternal life . . .

_____ _____

_____ _____

_____ _____

_____ _____

_____ _____

_____ _____

_____ _____

Eternal rest grant to them, O Lord, and let perpetual light shine upon them. May their souls, and the souls of all the faithful departed, by the mercy of God rest in peace. Amen.

Eternal rest grant to them, O Lord, and let perpetual light shine upon them. May their souls, and the souls of all the faithful departed, by the mercy of God rest in peace. Amen.

Eternal rest grant to them, O Lord, and let perpetual light shine upon them. May their souls, and the souls of all the faithful departed, by the mercy of God rest in peace. Amen.

Eternal rest grant to them, O Lord, and let perpetual light shine upon them. May their souls, and the souls of all the faithful departed, by the mercy of God rest in peace. Amen.

PART SIX
MY DAILY PRAYERS

Out of the depths I cry to you, O Lord!
Lord, hear my voice!
Let your ears be attentive
To the voice of my supplications!
If you, O Lord, should mark iniquities,
Lord, who could stand?
But there is forgiveness with you,
that you may be feared.
I wait for the Lord, my soul waits,
and in his word I hope.
my soul waits for the Lord
more than watchmen for the morning.

—Psalm 130:1–6

Daily Prayers

St. Paul urges us to "pray constantly" (1 Thessalonians 5:16). When we don't know what to say or how to approach God, traditional prayers from the treasury of the Church are a rich resource. Devotional prayers such as the Rosary or the Chaplet of Divine Mercy can be used to reflect on the life of Christ; they can also be personalized when we attach specific intentions to each part of the prayer. The Liturgy of the Hours is an ancient form of Christian prayer that helps us join our daily routines to the movements of the psalms. Litanies and novenas can help us call on specific saints for their intercession. The Examen from St. Ignatius of Loyola raises our awareness of the ways we are responding to God in our daily experience, and simple exercises for meditative prayer can help us contemplate God's presence with us. All of these traditional forms of prayer can be easily found with a simple search, or in collections such as *The Ave Treasury of Catholic Prayers*.

This section is reserved for you to record your favorite prayers for daily living. To "pray constantly" means turning to the Lord throughout the day and sharing what is on our hearts and minds. Below are some sample offerings as you move through your day, but you can write your own daily prayers here as well.

Morning Prayers

O Lord, in the morning you hear my voice.

—Psalm 5:3a

As I open my eyes, before I arise,
I give my day unto you, God.
For the blessings to come, I thank you.
For the challenges, too, I trust you.
Give me wisdom and strength just enough for the day,
so that in every way I please you. Amen.

Noontime Prayers

Give counsel,
grant justice;
make your shade like night
at the height of noon.

—Isaiah 16:3

At the height of the day, I take refuge in you, Lord.
When my burden is weary, you lighten my load.
When the way is confusing, please make straight the road.
Stay with me, Jesus. I stand here ready
to love you, to trust you, to thank you,
and to confess that I need you as much as my next breath. Amen.

Evening Prayers

So teach us to number our days
that we may get a heart of wisdom.

—Psalm 90:12

From dawn to dusk, you have been my light.
Lord, help me remember your gifts and my failings alike.
Have mercy, and grant me the grace I need
to see all the ways you've been with me today. Amen.

Bedtime Prayers

In peace I will both lie down and sleep;
for you alone, O Lord, make me dwell in safety.
—Psalm 4:8

Day is done; the night has come with sacred silence
to release us from all striving.
Search us, O God.
Teach us to love as you love, to forgive as you forgive.
And when at last we close our eyes,
send your angels to guard and protect us,
as you refresh us to begin again. Amen.

PART SEVEN
MY PRAYER INTENTIONS

Intention: Date:

Bible verses that help me during this time:

How do I sense God leading me through this?

Updates:

*Pay attention to the people God puts in your path if
you want to discern what God is up to in your life.*
—Henri Nouwen

Intention: Date:

Bible verses that help me during this time:

How do I sense God leading me through this?

Updates:

The more conscientious one is in becoming familiar with the sacred writings, the richer an understanding one will draw from them. . . .

Intention: Date:

Bible verses that help me during this time:

How do I sense God leading me through this?

Updates:

> . . . As with the earth, the more it is cultivated,
> the more abundant is its harvest.
> —St. Isidore of Seville

Part Seven: My Prayer Intentions

Intention: Date:

Bible verses that help me during this time:

How do I sense God leading me through this?

Updates:

Jesus for all, and all for Jesus.
—Bl. Rani Maria Vattalil

Intention: Date:

Bible verses that help me during this time:

How do I sense God leading me through this?

Updates:

> *I am not my own; I have given myself*
> *to Jesus. He must be my only love.*
> *—St. Kateri Tekakwitha*

Intention: Date:

Bible verses that help me during this time:

How do I sense God leading me through this?

Updates:

Souls without prayer are like people whose bodies or limbs are paralyzed: they possess feet and hands but they cannot control them. In the same way . . .

Intention: Date:

Bible verses that help me during this time:

How do I sense God leading me through this?

Updates:

. . . souls so infirm and so accustomed to busying themselves with outside affairs seem incapable of entering into themselves at all.
—*St. Teresa of Avila*

Intention: Date:

Bible verses that help me during this time:

How do I sense God leading me through this?

Updates:

Pray and God will do the rest.
—St. Josephine Bakhita

Intention: Date:

Bible verses that help me during this time:

How do I sense God leading me through this?

Updates:

We must pray.
—Servant of God Darwin Ramos

Intention: Date:

Bible verses that help me during this time:

How do I sense God leading me through this?

Updates:

We must approach our meditation realizing that "grace," "mercy," and "faith" are not permanent inalienable possessions which we gain by our efforts and retain as though by right, provided that we behave ourselves. . . .

Intention: Date:

Bible verses that help me during this time:

How do I sense God leading me through this?

Updates:

> . . . *They are constantly renewed gifts . . . renewed from moment to moment, directly and personally by God in his love for us.*
> —*Thomas Merton*

Part Seven: My Prayer Intentions

Intention: Date:

Bible verses that help me during this time:

How do I sense God leading me through this?

Updates:

Love is not blind. Love sees the weakness of the beloved and tries to shoulder his or her burdens.
—Ven. Francis Xavier Nguyễn Văn Thuận

Intention: Date:

Bible verses that help me during this time:

How do I sense God leading me through this?

Updates:

Whatever happens, behave in such a way that God will be glorified. . . . Be steadfast, and let us meet in heaven.
—St. Andrew Kim Taegon

Intention: Date:

Bible verses that help me during this time:

How do I sense God leading me through this?

Updates:

The devil dreads fasting, prayer, humility, and good works: He is not able even to stop my mouth who speaks against him. The illusions of the devil soon vanish, especially if a man arms himself with the Sign of the Cross. . . .

Intention: Date:

Bible verses that help me during this time:

How do I sense God leading me through this?

Updates:

*. . . The devils tremble at the Sign of the Cross of our Lord,
by which he triumphed over and disarmed them.
—St. Anthony Abbot*

Intention: Date:

Bible verses that help me during this time:

How do I sense God leading me through this?

Updates:

If we are to serve, if we are to care, if we are to minister, we have to get right inside.
— *Servant of God Thea Bowman*

Intention: Date:

Bible verses that help me during this time:

How do I sense God leading me through this?

Updates:

God is with me. I want nothing on earth.
—*Ven. Pierre Toussaint*

Intention: Date:

Bible verses that help me during this time:

How do I sense God leading me through this?

Updates:

One must not think that a person who is suffering is not praying. He is offering up his sufferings to God, and many a time he is praying much more truly . . .

Intention: Date:

Bible verses that help me during this time:

How do I sense God leading me through this?

Updates:

> . . . than one who goes away by himself and meditates his head off,
> and, if he has squeezed out a few tears, thinks that is prayer.
> —St. Teresa of Avila

Intention: Date:

Bible verses that help me during this time:

How do I sense God leading me through this?

Updates:

*God never tires of forgiving us; we are
the ones who tire of seeking his mercy.
—Pope Francis*

Intention: Date:

Bible verses that help me during this time:

How do I sense God leading me through this?

Updates:

*If you have lost the taste for prayer, you will regain
the desire for it by returning humbly to its practice.*
—St. Paul VI

Intention: Date:

Bible verses that help me during this time:

How do I sense God leading me through this?

Updates:

Nothing is more practical than finding God, than falling in love in quite an absolute, final way. What you are in love with, what seizes your imagination, will affect everything. It will decide what will get you out of bed in the morning, what you do . . .

Intention: Date:

Bible verses that help me during this time:

How do I sense God leading me through this?

Updates:

> . . . with your evenings, how you spend your weekends, what you read,
> whom you know, what breaks your heart, and what amazes you with
> joy and gratitude. Fall in love, stay in love, and it will decide everything.
> —Fr. Pedro Arupe, SJ

Intention: Date:

Bible verses that help me during this time:

How do I sense God leading me through this?

Updates:

*All shall be well, and all shall be well,
and all manner of thing shall be well.*
—Julian of Norwich

Intention: Date:

Bible verses that help me during this time:

How do I sense God leading me through this?

Updates:

For you, Jesus, if you want it, I want it, too.
—Bl. Chiara Badano

Intention: Date:

Bible verses that help me during this time:

How do I sense God leading me through this?

Updates:

The storm exposes our vulnerability and uncovers those false and superfluous certainties around which we have constructed our daily schedules, our projects, our habits, and priorities. . . .

Intention: Date:

Bible verses that help me during this time:

How do I sense God leading me through this?

Updates:

> . . . It shows us how we have allowed to become dull
> and feeble the very things that nourish, sustain, and
> strengthen our lives and our communities.
> —Pope Francis

Intention: Date:

Bible verses that help me during this time:

How do I sense God leading me through this?

Updates:

The life of prayer is the habit of being in the presence of the thrice-holy God and in communion with him.
—CCC *2565*

Intention: Date:

Bible verses that help me during this time:

How do I sense God leading me through this?

Updates:

May today there be peace within. . . . May you not forget the infinite possibilities that are born of faith.
—*St. Teresa of Avila*

Intention: Date:

Bible verses that help me during this time:

How do I sense God leading me through this?

Updates:

The essence of prayer is not the effort to make God give us something. Prayer, then, is not just informing God of our needs, for God already knows them. . . .

Intention: Date:

Bible verses that help me during this time:

How do I sense God leading me through this?

Updates:

. . . Rather, the purpose of prayer is to give God the opportunity to bestow the gifts He will give us when we are ready to accept them.
—Ven. Fulton Sheen

Intention: Date:

Bible verses that help me during this time:

How do I sense God leading me through this?

Updates:

*Prayer is the best weapon we possess.
It is the key that opens the heart of God
—St. Padre Pio*

Intention: Date:

Bible verses that help me during this time:

How do I sense God leading me through this?

Updates:

I am so sorely in need of prayer! In it rests all my hope and consolation.
—*Bl. Basil Moreau*

Part Seven: My Prayer Intentions

Intention: Date:

Bible verses that help me during this time:

How do I sense God leading me through this?

Updates:

I believe you are a personal God, and hear me when I speak, even my trivial petty speech. So I will tell you personally over and over I love you, I adore you, I worship you. . . .

Intention: Date:

Bible verses that help me during this time:

How do I sense God leading me through this?

Updates:

*. . . Make me mean it in my life. Make me show it by my choices.
Make me show it from my waking thought to my sleeping.
—Dorothy Day*

Intention: Date:

Bible verses that help me during this time:

How do I sense God leading me through this?

Updates:

> *Prayer is helplessness casting itself on power, infirmity leaning on strength, misery reaching to mercy, and a prisoner clamoring for relief.*
> —Ven. Fulton Sheen

Intention: Date:

Bible verses that help me during this time:

How do I sense God leading me through this?

Updates:

It is a beautiful and salutary thought that, wherever people are praying in the world, there the Holy Spirit is, the living breath of prayer.
—St. John Paul II

Intention: Date:

Bible verses that help me during this time:

How do I sense God leading me through this?

Updates:

*There is the prayer we each must offer to the Father quietly and alone.
We contemplate the living God, offering ourselves . . .*

Intention: Date:

Bible verses that help me during this time:

How do I sense God leading me through this?

Updates:

*. . . to be drawn into His love and learning
to take that same love to heart.*
—Constitutions of the Congregation of Holy Cross, no. 30

Part Seven: My Prayer Intentions

Intention: Date:

Bible verses that help me during this time:

How do I sense God leading me through this?

Updates:

If you follow Jesus' advice and pray to God constantly, then you will learn to pray well. God himself will teach you.
—St. John Paul II

Intention: Date:

Bible verses that help me during this time:

How do I sense God leading me through this?

Updates:

*Prayer is the encounter of God's thirst with ours.
God thirsts that we may thirst for him.*
—St. Augustine

Intention: Date:

Bible verses that help me during this time:

How do I sense God leading me through this?

Updates:

A desert watered by prayer grows and flourishes, takes on an air of joy and is adorned with delicious fruits, . . .

Intention: Date:

Bible verses that help me during this time:

How do I sense God leading me through this?

Updates:

> *. . . because it draws down the blessings*
> *of heaven on those who dwell there.*
> —Bl. Basil Moreau

Intention: Date:

Bible verses that help me during this time:

How do I sense God leading me through this?

Updates:

*Thou art the living flame . . . enter into me and
set me on fire after thy pattern and likeness.*
—St. John Henry Newman

Intention: Date:

Bible verses that help me during this time:

How do I sense God leading me through this?

Updates:

A soul arms itself by prayer for all kinds of combat.
—St. Faustina Kowalska

Part Seven: My Prayer Intentions

Intention: Date:

Bible verses that help me during this time:

How do I sense God leading me through this?

Updates:

Virtues are formed by prayer. Prayer preserves temperance. Prayer suppresses anger. . . .

Intention: Date:

Bible verses that help me during this time:

How do I sense God leading me through this?

Updates:

. . . Prayer prevents emotions of pride and envy. Prayer draws into the soul the Holy Spirit, and raises us to heaven.
—*St. Ephrem of Syria*

Part Seven: My Prayer Intentions

Intention: Date:

Bible verses that help me during this time:

How do I sense God leading me through this?

Updates:

Prayer is the unceasing recognition that God is wherever we are, always inviting us to come closer and to celebrate the divine gift of being alive.
—Henri Nouwen

Intention: Date:

Bible verses that help me during this time:

How do I sense God leading me through this?

Updates:

Prayer is in fact the recognition of our limits and our dependence: we come from God, we are of God, and to God we return.
—*St. John Paul II*

Intention: Date:

Bible verses that help me during this time:

How do I sense God leading me through this?

Updates:

*If one dream should fall and break into a thousand pieces . . .
never be afraid to pick one of those pieces up and begin again. . . .*

Intention: Date:

Bible verses that help me during this time:

How do I sense God leading me through this?

Updates:

. . . That's the beauty of being alive. . . .
We can always start all over again.
—St. Bernadette Soubirous

Intention: Date:

Bible verses that help me during this time:

How do I sense God leading me through this?

Updates:

The wish to pray is a prayer in itself.
—George Bernanos

Intention: Date:

Bible verses that help me during this time:

How do I sense God leading me through this?

Updates:

> *God is a spring of living water which flows*
> *unceasingly into the hearts of those who pray.*
> *—St. Louis de Montfort*

Intention: Date:

Bible verses that help me during this time:

How do I sense God leading me through this?

Updates:

If you ever feel distressed during your day, call upon Our Lady—just say this simple prayer: . . .

Intention: Date:

Bible verses that help me during this time:

How do I sense God leading me through this?

Updates:

> ... "Mary, Mother of Jesus, please be a mother to me now."
> I must admit, this prayer has never failed me.
> —St. Teresa of Calcutta

Intention: Date:

Bible verses that help me during this time:

How do I sense God leading me through this?

Updates:

Everything, even sweeping, scraping vegetables, weeding a garden, and waiting on the sick, could be a prayer if it were offered to God.
—St. Martin de Porres

Intention: Date:

Bible verses that help me during this time:

How do I sense God leading me through this?

Updates:

The biggest human temptation is to settle for too little.
—*Thomas Merton*

Part Seven: My Prayer Intentions

Intention: Date:

Bible verses that help me during this time:

How do I sense God leading me through this?

Updates:

This is how you pray continually—not by offering prayer in words, but by joining yourself to God . . .

Intention: Date:

Bible verses that help me during this time:

How do I sense God leading me through this?

Updates:

> . . . through your whole way of life, so that your life becomes
> one continuous and uninterrupted prayer.
> —St. Basil the Great

Part Seven: My Prayer Intentions

Intention: Date:

Bible verses that help me during this time:

How do I sense God leading me through this?

Updates:

Nothing so likens you to God, as to forgive him who has injured you.
—St. John Chrysostom

Intention: Date:

Bible verses that help me during this time:

How do I sense God leading me through this?

Updates:

Let us not grow tired of prayers—confidence works miracles.
—St. Thérèse of Lisieux

Intention: Date:

Bible verses that help me during this time:

How do I sense God leading me through this?

Updates:

*For I do not seek to understand in order that I may believe,
but I believe in order to understand. . . .*

Intention: Date:

Bible verses that help me during this time:

How do I sense God leading me through this?

Updates:

. . . For this also I believe—that unless I believe I shall not understand.
—St. Anselm

Intention: Date:

Bible verses that help me during this time:

How do I sense God leading me through this?

Updates:

Let us throw ourselves into the ocean of God's goodness, where every failing will be canceled and anxiety turned into love.
—St. Paul of the Cross

Intention: Date:

Bible verses that help me during this time:

How do I sense God leading me through this?

Updates:

*Every fall, even if it be grave and repeated, serves us always
and only as a little step toward a higher perfection.
—St. Maximilian Kolbe*

Intention: Date:

Bible verses that help me during this time:

How do I sense God leading me through this?

Updates:

*If the lungs of prayer and of the Word of God do not nourish
the breath of spiritual life, we risk suffocating . . .*

Intention: Date:

Bible verses that help me during this time:

How do I sense God leading me through this?

Updates:

. . . in the midst of a thousand daily cares. Prayer is the breath of the soul and of life.
—*Pope Benedict XVI*

Part Seven: My Prayer Intentions

Intention: Date:

Bible verses that help me during this time:

How do I sense God leading me through this?

Updates:

*Hold your eyes on God and leave the doing to him.
That is all the doing you have to worry about.
—St. Jane Frances de Chantal*

Intention: Date:

Bible verses that help me during this time:

How do I sense God leading me through this?

Updates:

He who goes about to reform the world must begin with himself.
—*St. Ignatius of Loyola*

Part Seven: My Prayer Intentions

Intention: Date:

Bible verses that help me during this time:

How do I sense God leading me through this?

Updates:

Prayer is still a little-known means; however, it is the most effective way to reestablish peace in our souls . . .

Intention: Date:

Bible verses that help me during this time:

How do I sense God leading me through this?

Updates:

. . . because it allows us to get ever closer to God's love.
—St. Maximilian Kolbe

Part Seven: My Prayer Intentions

Intention: Date:

Bible verses that help me during this time:

How do I sense God leading me through this?

Updates:

*Life is precious. Not because it is unchangeable
like a diamond, but because it is vulnerable.*
—*Henri Nouwen*

Intention: Date:

Bible verses that help me during this time:

How do I sense God leading me through this?

Updates:

*I know well that the greater and more beautiful the work is,
the more terrible will be the storms that rage against it.
—St. Faustina Kowalska*

Intention: Date:

Bible verses that help me during this time:

How do I sense God leading me through this?

Updates:

During painful times, when you feel a terrible void, think how God is enlarging the capacity of your soul . . .

Intention: Date:

Bible verses that help me during this time:

How do I sense God leading me through this?

Updates:

> . . . *so that it can receive him—making it, as it were, infinite as he is infinite.*
> —St. Elizabeth of the Trinity

Intention: Date:

Bible verses that help me during this time:

How do I sense God leading me through this?

Updates:

The soul always fears until she arrives at true love.
—*St. Catherine of Siena*

Intention: Date:

Bible verses that help me during this time:

How do I sense God leading me through this?

Updates:

When it comes to life the critical thing is whether you take things for granted or take them with gratitude.
—G. K. Chesterton

Part Seven: My Prayer Intentions

Intention: Date:

Bible verses that help me during this time:

How do I sense God leading me through this?

Updates:

Prayer is our faith attending to the Lord, and in that faith we meet him individually, . . .

Intention: Date:

Bible verses that help me during this time:

How do I sense God leading me through this?

Updates:

> *. . . yet we also stand in the company of
> others who know God as their Father.*
> —Constitutions of the Congregation of Holy Cross, no. 23

Intention: Date:

Bible verses that help me during this time:

How do I sense God leading me through this?

Updates:

Lord of all things, you see my heart, you know my desires.
—St. Agatha of Sicily

Intention: Date:

Bible verses that help me during this time:

How do I sense God leading me through this?

Updates:

> *Do not abandon yourselves to despair. We are an Easter people and hallelujah is our song.*
> —St. John Paul II

Intention: Date:

Bible verses that help me during this time:

How do I sense God leading me through this?

Updates:

For me, prayer is a surge of the heart; it is a simple look turned toward heaven, it is a cry of recognition and of love, embracing both trial and joy.
—St. Thérèse of Lisieux

Intention: Date:

Bible verses that help me during this time:

How do I sense God leading me through this?

Updates:

Prayer gives consistency and vitality to everything we do.
—Pope Francis

Intention: Date:

Bible verses that help me during this time:

How do I sense God leading me through this?

Updates:

One who has hope lives differently.
—Pope Benedict XVI

Intention: Date:

Bible verses that help me during this time:

How do I sense God leading me through this?

Updates:

Be good. Love the Lord. Pray for those who do not know him. It is a great grace to know God.
—*St. Josephine Bakhita*

Intention: Date:

Bible verses that help me during this time:

How do I sense God leading me through this?

Updates:

We must not be disturbed at our imperfections since for us perfection consists in fighting against them.
—St. Francis de Sales

Intention: Date:

Bible verses that help me during this time:

How do I sense God leading me through this?

Updates:

Your heart is greater than your wounds.
—Henri Nouwen

Intention: Date:

Bible verses that help me during this time:

How do I sense God leading me through this?

Updates:

You cannot love a thing without wishing to fight for it.
—G. K. Chesterton

Intention: Date:

Bible verses that help me during this time:

How do I sense God leading me through this?

Updates:

In my deepest wounds, I saw your glory, and it dazzled me.
—St. Augustine

Intention: Date:

Bible verses that help me during this time:

How do I sense God leading me through this?

Updates:

Continue to be patient; it will all be for your good.
—St. Padre Pio

Intention: Date:

Bible verses that help me during this time:

How do I sense God leading me through this?

Updates:

> *The more a soul loves, the more it longs,*
> *the more it hopes, the more it finds.*
> *—Fr. Jean-Pierre de Caussade, SJ*

Intention: Date:

Bible verses that help me during this time:

How do I sense God leading me through this?

Updates:

Each of us is the result of a thought of God. Each of us is willed. Each of us is loved. Each of us is necessary.
—Pope Benedict XVI

Intention: Date:

Bible verses that help me during this time:

How do I sense God leading me through this?

Updates:

I really only love God as much as I love the person I love the least.
—Dorothy Day

Part Seven: My Prayer Intentions

Intention: Date:

Bible verses that help me during this time:

How do I sense God leading me through this?

Updates:

*We grow in wisdom and maturity when we take
the time to touch the suffering of others.*
—Pope Francis

Intention: Date:

Bible verses that help me during this time:

How do I sense God leading me through this?

Updates:

Seek grace in the smallest things, and you will also find grace to accomplish, to believe in, and to hope for the greatest things.
—*St. Peter Faber*

Intention: Date:

Bible verses that help me during this time:

How do I sense God leading me through this?

Updates:

With the soul's eye fixed on eternity, struggle on.
—*Bl. Solanus Casey*

Intention: Date:

Bible verses that help me during this time:

How do I sense God leading me through this?

Updates:

Those who say they don't have time for prayer are not lacking time, but love.
—St. John Paul II

Intention: Date:

Bible verses that help me during this time:

How do I sense God leading me through this?

Updates:

There are five excellent qualities which are required in all prayer. Prayer must be confident, ordered, suitable, devout, and humble.
—St. Thomas Aquinas

Intention: Date:

Bible verses that help me during this time:

How do I sense God leading me through this?

Updates:

Prayer is the light of the soul.
—St. John Chrysostom

Intention: Date:

Bible verses that help me during this time:

How do I sense God leading me through this?

Updates:

If you would suffer patiently the adversities and miseries of life, be a person of prayer.
—St. Bonaventure

Intention: Date:

Bible verses that help me during this time:

How do I sense God leading me through this?

Updates:

Every single grace comes to the soul through prayer.
—St. Faustina Kowalska

Intention: Date:

Bible verses that help me during this time:

How do I sense God leading me through this?

Updates:

*Pray, hope, and don't worry. Worry is useless.
God is merciful and will hear your prayer.
—St. Padre Pio*

Intention: Date:

Bible verses that help me during this time:

How do I sense God leading me through this?

Updates:

*Men do not fear a powerful hostile army as the powers
of hell fear the name and protection of Mary.*
—St. Bonaventure

Intention: Date:

Bible verses that help me during this time:

How do I sense God leading me through this?

Updates:

When you feel the assaults of passion and anger, then is the time to be silent as Jesus was silent in the midst of his ignomies and sufferings.
—*St. Paul of the Cross*

Intention: Date:

Bible verses that help me during this time:

How do I sense God leading me through this?

Updates:

If you are yourself at peace, then there is at least some peace in the world. Then share your peace with everyone, and everyone will be at peace.
—Thomas Merton

Intention: Date:

Bible verses that help me during this time:

How do I sense God leading me through this?

Updates:

The secret to happiness is to live moment by moment and to thank God for all that he, in his goodness, sends to us day after day.
—St. Gianna Molla

Founded in 1865 by Fr. Edward Sorin, CSC, **Ave Maria Press** is an apostolate of the Congregation of Holy Cross, United States Province of Priests and Brothers. Ave is a nonprofit Catholic publishing ministry that serves the spiritual and formative needs of the Church and its schools, institutions, and ministers; Christian individuals and families; and others seeking spiritual nourishment.

Ave remains one of the oldest continually operating Catholic publishing houses in the country and a leader in publishing Catholic high school religion textbooks, ministry resources, and books on prayer and spirituality.

In the tradition of Holy Cross, Ave is committed, as an educator in the faith, to help people know, love, and serve God and to spread the gospel of Jesus Christ through books and other resources.

Ave Maria Press perpetuates Fr. Sorin's vision to honor Mary and provide an important outlet for good Catholic writing.

More Resources for Scripture Study and Prayer from Ave Maria Press

The Ave Catholic Notetaking Bible (RSV2CE)
Available in Hardcover and Imitation Leather

Living the Word Catholic Women's Bible (RSV2CE)
Living the Word Companion Journal
Available in Hardcover

The Ave Guide to Eucharistic Adoration

The Ave Guide to the Scriptural Rosary

The Ave Prayer Book for Catholic Mothers

The Ave Treasury of Catholic Prayers

Look for these titles wherever books and eBooks are sold.
Visit **avemariapress.com** to learn more.